The Choices You Make

The Choices You Make

Quotes by Walter E. Simendinger

Edited by
William E. Simendinger

iUniverse, Inc.
Bloomington

The Choices You Make

iUniverse books may be ordered through booksellers or by contacting:

iUniverse
1663 Liberty Drive
Bloomington, IN 47403
www.iuniverse.com
1-800-Authors (1-800-288-4677)

Because of the dynamic nature of the Internet, any Web addresses or links contained in this book may have changed since publication and may no longer be valid. The views expressed in this work are solely those of the author and do not necessarily reflect the views of the publisher, and the publisher hereby disclaims any responsibility for them.

ISBN: 978-1-4502-7348-0 (sc)
ISBN: 978-1-4502-7349-7 (ebk)

Library of Congress Control Number: 2010917467

Printed in the United States of America

iUniverse rev. date: 11/29/2010

Dedicated to Walter E. Simendinger

Walter Simendinger's business and personal philosophies are designed to make you highly successful. These are his words and can bring good fortune to your life.

Who has all the money?

If you want to get anything, you have to
go with someone who has something.

You become what you think about.

I thought about having
my own business.
It almost became an obsession for me.

I always had a job.

I hope we gave you a faith in
God that will last forever.

When you are on your own, the habits you developed will either serve you well or hold you down.

I hope you would learn to do anything from plumbing to wiring to car mechanics to bookkeeping so that making money was never a problem for you.

Make believe you earned every cent of your education. When you earn it – you are a little more careful on how you spend it.

The drink you would drink
would be a beer.

Its good to have a fallback list.

My role model was:

1. Independent

2. Entrepreneur

3. Smart

4. Knowledgable on how to invest

5. Knowledgable on how to make money.

Boy, I could do that.

Criteria for wife:
Beauty
Nurse

I read the Bible every morning.

I am really humbled by what we have done. Its only been by God's grace.

Two most important decision a person makes:

1. What they do with their life
2. Who they marry

I had 23 hours a day to work.

If you are working for a big company,
you have to do something to
put some light on yourself.

I saw a lot of opportunities for success.

I might not be as smart as the next guy, but I can outwork him.

I thought my car only worked on Mobil.

When buying real estate, regardless of whether or not a traffic light changes, a far corner at an intersection is open to get in and out.

I always had the knowledge
that if I was to die,
I would go to heaven.

Prayer has been a real backbone
of our love and faith.

The Bible teaches you
need to accept Christ
as your personal savior,
to be born again.
To enter the Kingdom of God.

Places to visit include:
Niagara Falls, Israel and Germany.

People generally buy gas getting on an interstate versus getting off.

To teach your children:
Start young
Take them to church.

I saw how easy people's career were ended and I wanted to have more security than that.

Can you imagine punks like us
owning a place like this?

You have to get a sheep skin.
A license to do something
that other people
are not allowed to do.

I just know I want it.

Everything is for sale.

I fixed it the next day.

I got my greatest achievement this year
when I now own my own backhoe.

You should imagine that someone just put a knife in your back. You need to take immediate action to stop the profuse bleeding.

There is nothing to worry about.

I want to review each account
that owes us money.

Which officer is going to be responsible
for approving credit and collecting
it and shutting off those that do
not pay according to terms?

That was the profession's loss.

Be careful you don't get your
teeth knocked out.

It doesn't take long to go from the top of the hill to the bottom of the hill.

I need you healthy.

You should become a doctor.

Lawyers should visit a prison and see where kids become professional cockroaches.

You're the best part of my day.

If there is a rotary, you have to place your gas station away from it.

I'm glad you are on my team.

Answering complaint letters sent to the executives of Mobil Oil Corporation was the hardest job I ever had.

Anything worth having is
worth working for.

Shovel the walk so it looks
like a king lives here.

No Way. I'm taking the boat
back. You can't get on the
lake for less than $5000.

The cop said I was packing a bigger piece than he was.

Learn to love the Lord.

If you ever marry a phlegmatic, you'll never get anything done, but you'll be the happiest people in the world.

People ask questions rationally
and buy emotionally.

You only get what you apply for.

We buy wholesale.

The kids have no idea what we do.

Be on your best behavior.

Don't fire your CPA until after
you have hired a new one.

If you build a house, it should be designed so everyone likes it. People who build funny looking houses have hard times selling them.

Can ' t

There is no greater burden
than a great potential.

Cucaracha

Don't park your car in the cash register.

Surround yourself with good people
and they will make you successful.

Be your own boss.

Its 5:00 am God, can I go
back to sleep now?

Look at current financial statements and ask:

1. How much money was generated in one month?

2. Who is getting their paws on the money first? Make me a list.

Help me achieve these goals.

In a big corporation, the rule is
Go Up and Out
As you climb the career ladder.

If you could run your business
1% smarter, how much
money would you make?

Your financial statement is your roadmap on where you are now and where you need to be in the future.

Do something you love
and
you will never work again in your life.

Is there a charge for this?

99% of all meetings are unnecessary.

I don't know where I am
going, but I am getting up.

There are no new gallons.

We made most of our money
buying houses, fixing them up
and then selling them.

It will be crooked until you fix it.

Motivate other people.

There is one in ten thousand chance of getting to the top of Mobil Oil Corporation.

60% of the people hate their work.

People are trapped by salary increases and then when they turn 55 the company lops their heads off.

Get a Godfather.

At the end of each month ask:
Did you make any money?
Where is it?

Pick a business:
Does it make lots of money?
Who runs it?

Motivation comes from a desire to eat.

Success is financial independence
and doing what you want.

Be a frugal spender.

Save 10% of your money.

Get into an industry that makes money.

Learn the business.
Work in it.
Know everything about it.

Find an exclusive location.

Be lucky.

I see these guys spend their whole lives working for companies taking each step in line until they turn 40 and decide to settle back on their salaries and enjoy life, and the company lops their head off and doesn't lose a step.

A lawyer can see a lot of deals
and opportunities where
he can make money.

I don't see myself as working.
I'm having a ball 16 hours a day.

Why do you resent anything
that resembles work?

Finish Strong.

Anything worth having is
worth working for.

Right now you are the chewee, but someday you will be the chewer.

A lazy attitude loses a lot
of opportunities
There are not many chances today.

You can't afford to make any mistakes when you are starting in business, or you will be done in.

Today you need credentials to get through the front door. Go for a CPA.

A bachelor of science is only as good as where it takes you.

What have you done for me lately?

Study accounting and law.

You need to learn an industry.

The only way to make a lot of money is in your own business.

Stay connected.